KIBEHO
An Epic Poem

N.B.J.Clayton

Copyright © N.B.J.Clayton, 2020

N.B.J.Clayton asserts the moral right to be identified as the owner of this work.

All rights reserved. No part of this publication may be reproduced, stored in a retrieval system, or transmitted in any form, by any means: electronic, mechanical, photocopying, recording or otherwise, without the prior permission of the copyright owner of this book.

This book is sold subject to the conditions that it shall not be resold, hired out or otherwise circulated, except in its original binding.

Publication data:

Kibeho: An Epic Poem, 1st ed.
ISBN 978 0 6487672 0 6

HIS027130 History/Military/Wars+Conflicts
POE023010 Poetry/Subject Themes/Death, Grief, Loss
POL061000 Political Science/Genocide+War Crimes

Book Cover Design by The Book Cover Whisperer:
ProfessionalBookCoverDesign.com

The Role of Infantry

To seek out and close with the enemy;
To kill or capture him;
To seize and hold ground;
To repel attack by day and night;
Regardless of season, weather, or terrain.

Citation

Do you know what death is?
Do you know what it smells like?

The following is based on actual events, occurring between April 17th and May 9th, 1995.

During the deployment of Australian Infantry troops to Rwanda, a vast number of tasks were performed: carrying stretchers through the AUSMED hospital; escorting dental technicians, medics and other specialised personnel through the winding hills of this land-locked country; and conducting security pickets on key installations to which were their sole responsibility – namely the hospital and barracks in Rwanda's capital, Kigali.

The basic infantryman was trained and prepared more for a situation as that presented by Vietnam, scaled down versions of the Falkland War and Somalia, or even a prolonged campaign against highly trained foes. During his deployment to Rwanda the training received seemed highly irrelevant and extraordinarily left-field: no one can be blamed for this. No one could fathom that their worst nightmare may actually bear its rancid fruit of toxicity.

- Intro -

The infantry stand to protect the medics who visit where laws lay absurd,
The hospital of United Nations that is here to protect and to serve,
A contradiction to humanity which serves to test the fabric of mind without cure,
Death and mutilation at every corner but a blur.

KIBEHO

- 1 -
One Australian soldier sees vivid decay,
For another the same appears this day,
For beyond their reach and affront to drench their honour,
Another victim is paraded to death amidst dolour.

- 2 -
An elderly man, looking to survive, is lead by this force of nature,
Two armed RPA pushing from behind, forcing lamb to slaughter,
Where machete combs the air to bend will and butcher,
No mark left but blood from torture.

- 3 -
The Rwandan Patriotic Army harbour ill-feeling,
They control the Hutu having commenced their reeling,
These soldiers of the devil have no empathy showing,
The Tutsi command over all with smiles and glowing.

- 4 -
The two Australians hence accept this fate,
The Hutu's death an unsavoury state,
Just another day amongst the decay,
They follow the orders of the day.

- 5 -
They turn to bunker and scrawl in diary of pain,
A document to scribe these crimes of ill-gain,
No good it will do, but try in strong voice spent,
Their feelings wild in a sieve-less vent.

- 6 -
One Aussie looks at his watch, it is time to eat,
A meal to be had but only this side of street,
The squalor around them gets put from mind,
They must survive even against this daily grind.

- 7 -
Life goes on but only for the evil,
Death comes to those that try to be peaceful,
The peacekeeper does not choose this roster for either,
They have no say and weapons neither.

- 8 -
Rules of Engagement stain the days,
The nights of endless fire from weapons abrupt and grey,
UN hands are tied against any retaliation,
They lack much ability amidst forced negation.

- 9 -
In peaceful barracks a Lieutenant Colonel sits,
Behind his desk with heavy mist,
Decisions here are murky at best,
For it is hard to try hard amongst the unrest.

- 10 -
A Major nods his head on receiving orders,
He must go to Kibeho, a place of decay and disorder,
The Virgin Mary did visit here aglow,
So the story goes and in it all know.

KIBEHO

- 11 -
A warning order is passed down to soldiers below,
For soldiers to embark by truck on the morrow,
To attend this place of fate and seclusion,
Where massacre will occur and starved of delusion.

- 12 -
Peacekeeping soldiers are happy with the order,
To do something decisive and away from the slaughter,
But they know not the fate of the day,
Which will unveil and reveal the devil at play.

- 13 -
The 18th of April is upon them within barrack's shield,
Early morning and screams come from further afield,
Someone being tortured and killed for the pleasure,
Tutsi hacking to death is as though strolling for leisure.

- 14 -
But to be ready for the journey they must prepare,
To Kibeho or bust to do their fair share,
To bring peace to this country, to give a real damn,
To do what they must in the face of this scam.

- 15 -
For peace is not in the nature of the Tutsi monster,
They say one thing but mean another,
They guise themselves as helpers and loyal,
Worthless creatures who seek only spoil.

- 16 -
And how many days and nights not right,
All filled with horrors and little delight,
How many victims to hospital gate,
How many days of hatred spate.

- 17 -
All are aghast at the waste of it all,
To help with one hand and then see patients fall,
Once departed from safe grounds the RPA do seek,
To engage in revenge upon those of the meek.

- 18 -
But the chance is near to change all without growl,
To turn evil into good and not throw in the towel,
To Kibeho or bust they will try and deliver a trust,
Which is short lived amid calamity and turns to rust.

- 19 -
The RPA are here, stationed of course,
Two-thousand strong with fear endorse,
At Kibeho they camp in lustful hate,
To concentrate all Hutu behind the gate.

- 20 -
The anniversary of the Rwandan massacre's date,
That is the importance of mind and set state,
That is the reason they are here today,
Not to help, but to hate beneath skies of darkening grey.

KIBEHO

- 21 -
The situation grows worse and worse,
Always needing but never a hearse,
The skies darken too from time to time,
The time is near for all to enter the grime.

- 22 -
Some children carry guns to look strong,
To sway judgement over the Hutu throng,
Younger than twelve and eight,
They monitor same gate.

- 23 -
All Hutu are treated poorly,
Children and women alike most surely,
Belongings destroyed and sustenance too,
Their humanity the Tutsi scorn as though shrew.

- 24 -
One twenty thousand IDPs all living as trash,
Internally Displaced Persons familiarly aghast,
How many will live to see the light of day,
So many have already seen the sun at last play.

- 25 -
A weapon is employed though only a little fire,
Only seventy-five rounds and that is not dire,
To say it's a relief is pure evil itself,
To see what is to come will put this to shelf.

- 26 -
Some people will say that all Aussies are lying,
Of the horrors before them and all of the dying,
Trying for purse of compensation's tether,
To dwell upon luxury of pension forever.

- 27 -
It delivers much mindful pain and suffering,
Inflicting great anxieties not worth remembering,
This is PTSD we speak of just waiting at door,
Mental anguish forever and more.

- 28 -
But this is all true and as true as the day,
I am not lying but take it as you may,
Though it matters not if some call this a lie,
For the truth is with us always and will never die.

- 29 -
What was it like and what was it to see,
Like meat on a table being cut up for thee,
With machete in hand, death after death you see,
RPA justice is delivered via mutilation and glee.

- 30 -
But let us not get too far ahead of ourselves here,
My writing is astray and should be pulled back a gear,
For we have not spoken of before this rancid test,
When in barracks at Kigali these good soldiers rest.

KIBEHO

- 31 -
Early afternoon and the order is given to mount,
To attend the camp and to check it all out,
By road the UN are to move like a gale,
To keep things secure and open the veil.

- 32 -
An interpreter is with them and lawyer as well,
To inspect the detention of prisoners of war as they swell,
For all the Hutu are convicted the same,
No honour in death and death is the game.

- 33 -
But they finally arrive in good grace at the gate,
Too many names to mention to date,
But their happiness is fading and fading so fast,
With distaste in mouth growing and minds aghast.

- 34 -
The minds of all are torched from within,
Rapidly engulfed by the dismay and the sin,
Of the entire camp, its humanity having faded away,
For it is nothing short of a camp in decay.

- 35 -
An RPA soldier stands in uniform at gate just spoke,
Scratching notes in diary a joke,
Looking the part as though making a play,
To help these poor people upon their way.

- 36 -
But he is here to clear out the camp,
Even with fist or with feet as they stamp,
To rid it of interahamwe as fast as he may,
And Hutu government loyalists who like to play.

- 37 -
The interahamwe are from government past,
When Tutsi invaders came in at last,
Those in power before the grass turned red,
No celebration of life but death in its stead.

- 38 -
The loyalists are a portion of enemy who stay,
Play hide and seek in order to fight another day,
Amongst the innocent they manipulate and hide,
Including Gendarmes who play to avoid the RPA tide.

- 39 -
The Hutu are civilians but appear more to some,
But they deny affiliation with interahamwe scum,
They are little more than victims at rest,
With life at stake in this test to be best.

- 40 -
The RPA are soldiers and Tutsi from true north,
They come in large number for what it is worth,
They come to invade and not here to tour,
To take back the country and much, much more.

KIBEHO

- 41 -
A power play of many here as you see,
But only one will be victor and others will flee,
Victory is also for those who do not whither,
To those who die fast with no pain to hinder.

- 42 -
So horrible to say,
When you see them prey,
Fast death mostly wished,
But for many is missed.

- 43 -
And Zambians too are here in number,
This is their post and muster,
Their parade ground for the world to see,
But victory is not to be.

- 44 -
Zambians of the UN are the best,
They have been here forever in test,
Or so it seems from the date of our arrival,
This is an admission and there is no denial.

- 45 -
Smoke fills the air from shanties and huts,
Huts galore built upon ground not struts,
No shrubs or trees to be seen from anywhere near,
One twenty thousand stand ground in fear.

- 46 -
Shots are fired in haste up ahead,
To get to the area Aussie carefully tread,
The crowd sees the Aussies arriving,
Now on foot instead of driving.

- 47 -
They watch as the Aussies approach the scene,
Where shooting was most surely obscene,
To find little evidence remaining,
For the RPA are quick and lack refraining.

- 48 -
Fast with machete and quick with wit,
They do well here to satisfy their habit,
They do not relent or lack dash,
When it comes to being rash.

- 49 -
Two Zambians walk past crowd and around,
On way to burial pit in ground,
Mass graves the order of the day,
More to come and here to stay.

- 50 -
Over shoulder another UN vehicle does appear,
And comes to a stop as it gets near,
One twenty thousand congregated in area small,
Scheming RPA having forced donkeys to stall.

- 51 -
But these people are not donkeys, nor stupid or grey,
Not docile or unimaginative but still they stay,
Forced to save their families and young,
The babies suckling and soon to be none.

- 52 -
Not a smile seen upon black face or white,
But occasional song can be heard as it might,
The church on the hill, a memory from past,
When the Virgin Mary did visit upon mast.

- 53 -
Two men are then seen of RPA cast,
Chasing an elderly man rather fast,
Machete in hand and ready to kill,
They catch their quarry and drag him to hut for thrill.

- 54 -
What can the Aussie do but watch in dismay,
Too far to investigate and too many displaced in the way,
To get there and look is pointless to say,
They can do little, war crimes having command over day.

Many disciplinary upsets were met by the keen eye of the infantry soldier in this segment of his life, which was far different to that for which he had trained so hard.

He wasn't fighting a war, but war was evident; he didn't get to fire his steyr or pistol, but weapons from all around lashed out their evil; and he never killed a sole, but the bodies were all around and piling higher. All he could do was report an incident, only permitted to deploy 'passive' preventative measures if human rights were being violated and only under specific situations (our Rules of Engagement), and not permitted to fire any weapon unless under dire circumstances (literally, self-defence); you might imagine the disgust felt by all. *So long ago, I hardly know.*

Initiative and common sense were to be the main weapons of this deployment.

Common sense is derived from the mind, is it no wonder then, that the mind should bear the brunt of all excessive anxiety and feeling.

PLEASE NOTE:

CCP can be identified as either:
Casualty Collection Point
or
Casualty Clearing Post

You decide.

- 55 -
All UN now watch, but never at rest,
Many small huts with blue sheeting donated by West,
Non Government Organisations here to do their best,
Also fall short of commanding over this Hutu Nest.

- 56 -
Another burst of fire from weapon is heard,
Aussie investigate once more, which sounds absurd,
What can they do when they get there at last,
Nothing at all but report it, as per the past.

- 57 -
Some tasks are fruitless and hard to fathom,
Carrying bodies to pit and burying without anthem,
Too many to count but it is a start,
Mutilated and hacked, with some falling apart.

- 58 -
An IDP man is pushed to the ground,
Sent on his way to Butare with laughter abound,
His family crying for him as he is forced along,
The wife and kids frustrated but strong.

- 59 -
Another RPA post further along,
Notice the man walking away from the throng,
They shoot him down dead as they feel they are best,
The body to be carried away and to join with the rest.

- 60 -
An RPA soldiers looks over a unimog truck,
The Aussie camel of country struck,
He wants to look in the cabin, to do a search,
He is forced aside and set upon perch.

- 61 -
How ugly that is to say,
How the soldiers can be stopped to look this way,
But he is free to command and free to destroy,
The good people around that do nothing to annoy.

- 62 -
It is the laws of the West,
Laws associated with what we deem best,
Too many organisation partitioning for justice and grace,
But such justice gathers bad moss and has no real face.

- 63 -
The UN is forced to play into the hand of law and order,
Which sees great crimes committed like thunder,
The lightning strikes as though from nowhere,
Nothing to do but suffer the consequences unfair.

- 64 -
They remember Malcolm Fraser's daughter of years before,
Going off at the men in a truck well armed from good store,
"What do you need them for? They are no good here,"
They are a deterrent to which common sense we adhere.

KIBEHO

- 65 -
An IDP is followed far from behind and executed in bad taste,
One is escorted past gate and forced upon way to Butare in haste,
Water containers are punctured, burst to force them along,
Some make it to tree line, others jumped upon by military throng.

- 66 -
Orders are later given to retreat and Aussie must obey,
It is too violent here to stay beyond the last light of day,
All think they are soldiers and here to stay,
But are forced to flee like cowards where IDP lay.

- 67 -
On the trucks they sit for most of the day,
They do as ordered despite what future will say,
Looking to intervene where atrocity rose its ugly stare,
To be forced to part with sanity under full glare.

- 68 -
But one last small victory can be seen quite near,
The Special Air Service have unscathed boy in ambulance rear,
They tie him up smoothly with bandages in pretence to mend,
And lie to the RPA that to hospital he must attend.

- 69 -
One of many whom made it to freedom and we trust,
An orphan to live long and held from the dust,
He made it to safety and orphanage sturdy,
Let us pray and hope he turned out to be worthy.

- 70 -
Back at Aussie Contingent HQ they prepare for the day,
The remainder of the platoon to be on their way,
To Kibeho or bust is their motive and conviction,
They must be on the move immediately and without restriction.

- 71 -
Infantry sections and full quota of medical staff prepare,
All the equipment and bandages to last, with none to spare,
Tarps and many stretchers are brought from store,
All prepared for weeks and thought of before.

- 72 -
Engineers too are there in seat front,
To travel afar with the grunt,
Waiting in unimog and then to Kibeho to greet,
To help with the poorly and many sick to treat.

- 73 -
Several more SAS troopers and Warrant Officer true,
All are here and stick together like glue,
Each and all to do the job he is told,
Or to do as he knows is required and bold.

- 74 -
When they finally arrive they too are aghast,
At the situation of the camp as with the past,
By far the worst camp seen to date,
It is clearly in an extremely bad state.

KIBEHO

- 75 -
It is a crisis to be sure, and home grown,
No mistake to be had or mentally sewn,
It is a shame that humanity is like this here,
They would do well if to laws adhere.

- 76 -
The infantry major here is of good grammar,
He approaches some RPA at post in good manner,
The evil in them can be seen as he steps forward,
They do not want the UN here as it is awkward.

- 77 -
He strolls past them without a word,
But their eyes seem to penetrate like a sword,
The Major is looking for a good ally,
And to the Zambians here he can surely rely.

- 78 -
Zambian Headquarters is shown him at last,
Allowed to enter and in good language vast,
He seeks one in command and holds out his hand,
A smiling face greets him as an old friend grand.

- 79 -
Medical staff give orders for all equipment,
To set up quickly, a post to give treatment,
A place to correctly treat against the peril,
All the victims of this civil war turned evil.

- 80 -
The RPA commander sees the work going ahead,
He is not happy but is aghast instead,
He wants the Hutu dead and not on the loose,
He wants them corralled with necks in a noose.

- 81 -
"You can't unpack here," is translated first rate,
The interpreter speaks well and in good state,
"You must not stay here, this is our ground, you see,
These people are ours and we will attend to thee."

- 82 -
"Where can we set up?" the Aussie does ask,
"Over there be good to entrust your task,"
To then be scrutinized in ugly way once again,
Equipment is dismantled after set up in vain.

- 83 -
Another RPA approaches quite fast,
"You cannot unpack here," he says at last,
"But we were advised this to be our place of stay,
To set up here has been decreed as okay."

- 84 -
"You must move at once," and so move they do,
To another spot more deluded than the previous two,
But on completion it only meets with the trend,
And to move again they must attend.

KIBEHO

- 85 -
Again the Aussie is ordered to move,
But stand their ground they must finally prove,
"We will not move again and tell your commander that,"
A weapon is seemingly pointed at Aussie commander in hat.

(86 -
"You must move for you cannot stay,"
"But your very commander said it was okay,"
"He is not here and I now give the order to thee,"
"Then do as you must for I do not agree."

- 87 -
The weapon and tension is lowered a gear,
"Okay, you can stay here, but do not interfere,
This is not your country of stay,"
Looking through their eyes the UN is like prey.

- 88 -
Another Zambian then introduces himself to the Major,
A good man who shoulders much favour,
They both fight their way through the swarm of humanity,
To find a makeshift morgue devoid of all sanity.

- 89 -
"These are the bodies from the night before,
When IDP were massacred by machete law,
It is common occurrence at this door,
To see many dead adorn the floor."

- 90 -
And so conviction of mind stands the Major well,
They will not be moved ever more in damned hell,
That is his word and stand by it he will,
So the Aussie can do his duty to the fill.

- 91 -
Story is then told of the Virgin Mary here,
In November '81 she did first appear,
The vision was apparition of events in store,
Until '82 appeared several times more.

- 92 -
There was a river of blood, it was here,
From this place called Kibeho all fear,
A massacre to occur and soon to be sure,
All were tense and believed in this gore.

- 93 -
The IDP praise the Virgin Mary's grace,
Trust her to protect them from mournful face
The Zambians and Aussies are here as mates,
To ensure their safety, some believe in the dates.

- 94 -
The main date is coming fast,
Will be upon them like unwanted task,
Sooner than they think a disgraceful show,
But never wanting it to blossom and grow.

KIBEHO

- 95 -
The Major takes leave and sees Captain of evil again,
The RPA commander of great sin and great stain,
For his manner is strongest and strangest of all,
Never wanting to help but only to sting and to maul.

- 96 -
"Everything is under control here Major, so be on your way,
You are not needed here and this is what I say,
Clear out why you have chance, for chances are few,
This is our country, and from its bosom we all grew."

- 97 -
The Major is concerned but is here to amend,
"We are here to help, at last, and to the very end,
To help as many as we may,
Even if skies are turning grey,"

- 98 -
"Go now Major, before it is too late,
We will attend the Hutu we hate,
We will tend this problem of past,
These Hutu we hate to the very last,"

- 99 -
"What Hutu problem is that of which you speak?"
The Major announces from beneath his hat and his peak,
"They need our help and our assistance,
Not our distaste or our ignorance."

- 100 -
The RPA commander expresses bane,
His true colours made clear and plain,
"We have all under control regards these Hutu at bay,
We shall deal quickly with Kibeho during our stay."

- 101)
The commander continues as he may,
"You think you know all, but nay,
The UN not know the time of day,
They know nought of this play."

- 102 -
The commander walks off when he sees at last,
The equipment of sanctuary unloaded hence ending the task,
The medical staff helping where they are sent,
But few IDP trust the Aussie at present.

- 103 -
Orders are then given for tour to be made around,
Circumnavigate the extremity of ground,
Check the vicinity outside the disorder,
See if anything further needs to be put to shoulder.

- 104 -
The CCP is finally set up and running,
But RPA inflict rules and victims are frowning,
They cannot get treated for wounds here and now,
The RPA are watching and grow stern at the brow.

- 105 -
And those that are treated do not last long,
RPA make visits with strung words most strong,
The Hutu move away from the care being provided,
In fear for their lives, seemingly soon to be ended.

- 106 -
And so the Aussie pulls play with medical treatments and tags,
Many medics under protection making visits with bags,
Going around the camp here and there,
Providing assistance as well they can under Tutsi stare.

- 107 -
And before the end of the day, the IDP no longer embalmed,
They start to come for help as is needed, and calmed,
They are given first aid and some transported away,
To hospital or other and prevented to stray.

- 108 -
The RPA looks on aghast as they must,
The Hutu are getting away leaving dust,
They are being aided instead of subdued,
This will not do and will not be approved.

- 109 -
Generators are active and running able,
Stretchers are employed and system stable,
The infantry do all they can,
And medics supervise to the man.

- 110 -
Carry this one here and that one there,
This one is dead so give him last stare,
This one is okay but this one real sick,
Take that mother and baby child to Kigali real quick.

- 111 -
The day draws to a close for all relieved medic,
And Infantry prepare to leave in one stick,
Get away before night is the order of day,
Come back tomorrow for another short stay.

- 112 -
And comes next day,
Not quite May,
April near end,
They follow the trend.

- 113 -
The morning breeze and a day to be grieved,
The day so vicious it will not be believed,
Many will look at this as illusion,
But coming fast is blunt conclusion.

- 114 -
The IDPs are bewildered and sodden,
Such a ghastly place it does not look modern,
The people are shells of former selves,
And empathy within all whom see just swells.

KIBEHO

- 115 -
The West feel the pain and do all they can,
The RPA desist and stick to the plan,
They want Hutu hurt and Interahamwe purged from turf,
They wish them all dead and huts scorched to the earth.

- 116 -
The evil keeps the IDPs at bay,
Not allowing them chance for hospital stay,
The courageous female Captain of medics does attack,
And calls upon all medics to drag IDP back.

- 117 -
From death's door they are saved or temporarily stalled,
Many now walk the road to Butare unscathed, not mauled,
They are given medical aid as they are forced upon their way,
No longer in camp and leaving behind silent cheers of hooray.

- 118 -
Some are given good medicines not rot,
Others treated well and given aid on the spot,
Some given aid as they continue the journey,
Along that dreary road by foot and not gurney.

- 119 -
And reprieve is caught by a few with good luck,
Whom receive an ambulance trip back from the muck,
Or on the back of unimog to safety in number,
Or orphanage for children no longer just lumber.

- 120 -
An RPA soldier tries to intervene,
"What are you doing to these people obscene?"
"Giving them treatment as well as deserved,
They are people and that meaning is not reserved."

- 121 -
"To be given first aid where aid can be given,
To be treated with good grace as written,
We are staff of medical profession,
And give all we can to help with our mission."

- 122 -
The RPA do not see this and have hate in the eye,
They are evil to the last and that is no lie,
They aggravate the Captain of medics to last,
Who gives them a lesson with a blast.

- 123 -
"You can not interfere with us this day,
Get out of our way so we can treat as we may,
We will help these people for as long as the day,
This is my vow, that we are here to stay."

- 124 -
And the day appears good, where treatments are given,
The tide is turning and sick are not beaten,
Their fear abating, they seek out first aid,
More and more search for this medical maid.

KIBEHO

- 125 -
It is becoming clearer as day continues to grow,
That the IDPs are courageous and now all know,
They are the meek and trodden on from above,
And yet many desist and continue their struggle for love.

- 126 -
They pray to the lord for safe keeping and help,
Some calls are answered with heartfelt yelp,
There were so many failures all around,
But now so many victories coming to ground.

- 127 -
The Captain is called upon in person to attend,
A woman with children is sick to the end,
The Zambian is afraid for fear she will die,
So Captain comes running with bag held high.

- 128 -
She has another medic in tow,
Someone with bag and medicines aglow,
They will look her over and do what they can,
Not to let her die and mass grave is ban.

- 129 -
There is a pregnant woman with two children close by,
She is in much pain with pity in eye,
She fears for her life and the life of her young,
Her baby unborn and unfortunately strung.

- 130 -
The baby is dead but inside the womb,
What to do but act quick to withhold the gloom,
The children beside her will be taken aside,
The woman by chopper for it is the fastest ride.

- 131 -
And that is a small victory for Aussie is gaining,
For patients are coming as though it is raining,
And then a complaint from RPA arrives,
They are unhappy and with great interference they strive.

- 132 -
RPA say: "The move from Kibeho is too slow," with a grin,
Medical treatment on road is conveying a sin,
It is not helpful to him for the UN to do it this way,
So Aussie commander of infantry comes into play.

- 133 -
The platoon commander comes up with idea if he may,
And talks to captain to get it underway,
"Will you agree if we treat them at post,
Before they engage road and to Butare for most."

- 134 -
"But you must not stop the flow or slow it at all,
But they can be treated if quick and do not stall,"
So five minutes a piece, no more is agreed,
Each individual treated as well as they need.

KIBEHO

- 135 -
Aussies making ground,
Medics treating those around,
Hutu moving through the post more readily,
Being instilled with great confidence more easily.

- 136 -
And a burst of fire then appears to rattle the air,
Many rounds fired from weapon unfair,
So again the infantry attend the ground,
And have a good look and see all around.

- 137 -
It takes time to get to where they are going,
The crowd too thick and rather knowing,
By the time the good soldiers get to do their search,
The remains have been removed from the crowd as people lurch.

- 138 -
Moments later a chopper is witnessed,
Approaching from Kigali as best can be guessed,
General Tousignant is here and appears in good state,
To give a speech to the throng and help them safely vacate.

- 139 -
He has a quick tour and sees all the dead,
More concerned than immediately read,
His face is sculptured art and a face of rock,
He looks to all as one born of this stock.

- 140 -
It's a glare from a soldier, do you hear,
One with experience to behold most dear,
But experience may be deferred by those quite near,
For what they see does not provide for good cheer.

- 141 -
For good cheer can not be found,
It is trodden in the ground,
The look of extensive experience is here read,
But not with a frown of forehead upon head.

- 142 -
A stare of hate but no upturned lip,
No wit can be seen or let slip,
It is a face of torture with no visible pain,
A stare of long distance for no real gain.

- 143 -
This is the stare of one who has seen too much,
Too much hatred which is hindrance and crutch,
It is experience through and through,
It can not be confused with anything and in that all knew.

- 144 -
To one who beholds it,
They hold it like true grit,
They can not let it go,
If you own it you are in the know.

- 145 -
Tousignant moves amongst the crowd around,
He takes it all in with bodyguards standing ground,
He then gives a speech on how the IDP should leave,
But leave they do not in tune with all they grieve.

- 146 -
Their safety is of greatest concern,
For them to depart is a lesson to learn,
But teaching is hard even through goodwill,
The IDP trust few and it is hard to instil.

- 147 -
So General departs in chopper as people rush forward,
It takes to the air as a few are skewered,
Shots from rifles seem to sing out from far and near,
A few good Hutu are killed as though deer.

- 148 -
Will the speech do any good,
Maybe if fully understood,
But eight dead men,
Is better than ten.

- 149 -
The Public Relations Officer for Aussie contingent stands,
With hidden camera in his hands,
A medic sees him playing with photographic ability,
And approaches with fastest mobility.

- 150 -
"If you are caught we will all die,
You must put it away, that is no lie,"
But he insists: "Just a minute more should be agreed,
For I have nearly finished with my need."

- 151 -
"Now damn it!" came out as a great knock,
And officer obeys with great shock,
And just in time as the door bursts open,
RPA soldiers looking for Hutu persons believed rotten.

- 152 -
Once they have gone the Major relents,
"Thank you Sergeant for all you, to me, have sent,
Your words were strong but served us both well,
Thank you from me, from bottom of well."

- 153 -
Later still and another chopper arrives from over the hill,
It carries Mr. Khan of the UN who carries no thrill,
A man on a mission and steadfast in conviction,
He will do all he can to ensure safe eviction.

- 154 -
Mr. Khan is to talk with RPA, with voice,
To display great character and tell them they have little choice,
The RPA must allow the UN to do its job here,
To help the unfortunate and able to do it without sneer.

KIBEHO

- 155 -
And the sky becomes grey and starts to turn nasty,
There is a storm on the horizon and it will be hasty,
It starts to rain, but lightly at first,
But it will grow to become the worst.

- 156 -
The time of day is drawing to close,
Things turn nasty as more is dispose,
Firing is heard upon the approaching dark,
The sky turning over in tune with the firing bark.

- 157 -
A soldier brings news of six priority one,
So medics come on the double: at the run,
They will attend their need, be careful and fair,
Task supplied to ambulance, to give aid in this lair.

- 158 -
Another comes to air of sucking chest,
A wound too serious for some to digest,
Commander of medical staff calms all down,
She is a gift from God and should be renown.

- 159 -
Infantry commander gets signaller aside,
He must set to task and prepare a ride,
A chopper is decided for chest and more,
The priority one whom can't wait, that's sure.

- 160 -
The chest and a broken femur take the lead,
Other wounded showing no greed,
Each organised in condition most worse,
In order to prevent death from enacting its curse.

- 161 -
Security party is given a task,
Prepare the evac area and no need to ask,
Just do their jobs as best they can,
Amongst the evil RPA scan.

- 162 -
And not long in the wait,
The chopper arrives in good state,
It is loaded real fast,
And returns to Kigali like last.

- 163 -
And it is time to go,
For sun is no longer aglow,
And to administration area they do retreat, not saunter,
Soon after a message is received, as 200 more meets slaughter.

- 164 -
They tie their heads to ground,
Sleeping bags around,
They do not sleep tonight,
There are too many dreams of fright.

- 165 -
And the morrow will see the CCP flee,
To the Zambian compound retreat for thee,
Where room is had in this place quite eerie,
Medics and infantry to help the weary.

- 166 -
And this morning will tell a story,
Of one which is most gory,
Do not read further if you are easily made ill,
For it is a story of many RPA as they kill.

Intel gathered during the legal officer's four-day tour was seen as a minor victory against the RPA oppression.

And then arrived the malignant dawning: the day of days:

> Saturday 22nd April, 1995.

KIBEHO

- 167 -
Do not cry as you read this today,
But bad dreams accompany as they may,
Draw from these words the solemn truth,
Of the horror to befall all here, nail and tooth.

- 168 -
The day already heated under cloudy sky,
The day to test many, especially the shy,
Much will change on the face of men steel,
As in women too change in how they feel.

- 169 -
Many dead from the night before,
Carried to harbour in ground galore,
Zambians have been busy all night,
Trying to bring what is wrong to right.

- 170 -
Stretcher parties organised for the task ahead,
Finding the living and others dead,
The dead to the ground to fester,
Amongst the living no jester.

- 171 -
Some must be left to die,
Limited medical supplies deny,
No peaceful sleep for the dying,
Nought can be done but not for lack of trying.

- 172 -
Casualty Collection Point is now the mention,
Another of many tasks requiring attention,
Clear the priority one away as fast as you can,
Keep others monitored and under visual scan.

- 173 -
Those nearing death await their place in the ground,
Priority one seats are few to be found,
Treat those whom can be treated sounds quite absurd,
But this is the truth and it must be heard.

- 174 -
100 victims are the minimum they count,
Victims of machete and bullet just mount,
All must be sorted and treated the same,
Could this possibly be nothing but an insane game.

- 175 -
The RPA keep killing,
And butchering willing,
The UN gathers the mess,
And do well under stress.

- 176 -
A woman sits with back against wall,
Her lower jaw and nose ready to fall,
Cleaved from her face,
It is a disgrace.

KIBEHO

- 177 -
Massive cuts to arms and legs,
Bullet wound to abdomen begs,
Chest and head wounds here to stay,
More mass graves the order of the day.

- 178 -
Triage set up near,
Get infantry into gear,
Get stretchers working hard,
They do not retard.

- 179 -
Massive gun wound to chest,
SAS medic has done his best,
The Hutu man will not live long,
He is sapped and no longer strong.

- 180 -
Faeces falls through mattress upon which he's lying,
The man loses control for he is near dying,
Human waste is thick as can be,
It is not something anyone wishes to see.

- 181 -
The shit from the near dying is disgusting at best,
But they shit as they die, as when at rest,
Disease is an issue made all the worse,
The Aussies try not to reflect on this curse.

- 182 -
Outside the children sift through shit,
Grabbing corn kernels and all they can fit,
To be boiled in container what they find on the ground,
To be eaten again to all are astound.

- 183 -
They eat the soles too of leather shoes,
Boiling them first despite their woes,
For food is so short in its supply,
There is none to be had, so eat shit and shoes, or die.

- 184 -
The people are starving but water is had,
Rain buckets from all sources mad,
They strive to gather what they can,
The RPA like not this plan.

- 185 -
So RPA stab the containers filled,
They take so rain cannot be milled,
Nothing left for the hungry,
Nothing for RPA but to be angry.

- 186 -
Men and women of the UN do moral duty,
But it is too much despite abilities most sturdy,
They cannot cope with this disaster,
To call Mass Casualty Clearance is just nature.

KIBEHO

- 187 -
The signaller sends message as soon as told,
The MCC is the strength and is bold,
The news hits the Aussie hospital at Kigali,
And they are calm and collective as they rally.

- 188 -
The cavalry are on their way,
Not a single one will stray,
They will come to the rescue,
And help clean all residue.

- 189 -
The infantry respond true to heart,
The beginning of day this is but the start,
Stretcher party here and another there,
Infantry galore ferrying patients aware.

- 190 -
Leave some dead where they lay,
They can be sorted later in day,
See to the living,
Strive to be giving.

- 191 -
A 40-something man looks glum,
Gunshot wound to sternum,
No exit wound can be seen,
Other than entry it appears clean.

- 192 -

Glucose and sodium provided,
The patient has not responded,
A stethoscope brings no lucidity,
Morphine to be used now a rarity.

- 193 -

Captain of medics is called over,
A little older and bolder,
The bullet has ruptured the aorta,
Another victim to slaughter.

- 194 -

The drip has increased blood volume,
This one is out of costume,
"It is not your fault at play,
Just how pans out the day."

- 195 -

Sergeant takes the man's hand,
Holds it in a death not grand,
"Goodbye to you I say,
I am sorry to have let you stray."

- 196 -

And then to more patients he must attend,
More patients than anyone can mend,
Victims young and old,
This is the story that must be told.

- 197 -
A six year old girl,
Her hair has a slight curl,
Machete wound to arm as though wood,
From RPA in courteous mood.

- 198 -
Another one with gunshot to upper arm,
Another with face sliced to harm,
Another brought in from outside,
But the last cannot be abide.

- 199 -
SAS guy says: "Take that gentleman back out please,"
Infantry responds with: "Please do not tease,"
"There are too many here,"
"Please do not jeer,"

- 200 -
SAS again: "Listen to what I say,
It is too late for him this day,
Place him outside against the wall,
His life will soon stall."

- 201 -
"We can only save those we can save,
The others are destined for the grave,
Leave him be, let him die,
We have limited supply."

- 202 -
"We have enough stock to save some,
I do not wish to sound glum,
I do not like to give the nod,
I do not like to play God."

- 203 -
"But decisions must be made,
Treat those whom can be laid,
Laid to hospital bed or better,
Be returned home and not fetter."

- 204 -
And so touring the field where wounded lay stranded,
It's a matter of pick and choose who shall be granted,
The chance to live on and hopefully be free,
Of this detestable place even the insane wouldn't like to see.

- 205 -
Some firing can be heard in the distance,
Bodies pricked as though with knight's lance,
Mostly machete attack at this supposed place of rest,
Hot and bloody go Aussie to the test.

- 206 -
But with all the hate and death this day,
Far far worse is yet to follow morning's play,
Far far far worse is yet to steer its ugly head,
Far far far far worse if left, yet to be read.

- 207 -
Around the few fallen, the medics tour,
Making Godly choices all the more,
"That one can be left, but take that one now,
Do as I tell you good soldier and do not row."

- 208 -
So infantry set to task,
With voice restrained behind mask,
They are starting to learn real fast,
And do as requested to last.

- 209 -
A victim has been attacked at the neck and face,
Breathing is hard and he is falling from grace,
Gasping for air through hole in his neck,
He looks and struggles as a true wreck.

- 210 -
"He will not live, I don't think,
I am tired of this place and this stink,"
Worse and worse by the hour,
But this is just a little rain as light shower.

- 211 -
"Give him priority one evacuation,"
So place on chopper provided with illation,
Sometimes compassion must to admitted,
Even though a greater sin may have been committed.

- 212 -
The dying man may have taken a seat, sure,
Someone else may have needed it more,
He may not be saved, but comfort is measured,
His death will be better than most have suffered.

- 213 -
A soldier is called and comes inside,
"Help us here for we are busy with the tide,
Take those two bodies and place in the gutter,
Line them up neatly with all of the other."

- 214 -
Another medic goes amongst all the deceased,
They are short on supplies and of these bodies released,
With no bandages left in medical bags,
The old must be returned from dead in rags.

- 215 -
"Wash these bandages for we are in need,
Use them again we have all agreed,
The patients may die from germs breeding,
But not from over bleeding."

- 216 -
"We must take all the chances we can,
We must fight to the very last man,
We must help as many as we can save,
And avoid sending them to the grave."

- 217 -
And the tasks continue throughout the morning,
Fixing bodies and shipping them from mooring,
From CCP berth and this miserable place,
To orphanage and hospital they race.

- 218 -
But this is still just a shower,
Not real rain from great tower,
Just a few wounded and dying,
Just wait and see if I'm lying.

- 219 -
The task so far as been easy,
Maybe a bit bloody and greasy,
But the real work is yet to play out,
The real Kibeho has not yet to give shout.

- 220 -
A chopper lands on the ground,
Many patients awaiting around,
They are loaded and off they fly,
And so goodbye to more supply.

- 221 -
Captain of medics returns to post,
Left for a second at the most,
A drip is seen in flesh of one dead,
It can also be used again or wasted instead.

- 222 -
"Get that drip and bandage as well, from floor,"
Sergeant gives voice: "It cannot be used more,"
"We have nothing left and so have to try,
I will not stand here and let everyone die."

- 223 -
And that is the order as morning does sit,
RPA attack as they see fit,
Patients awarded chopper or not,
Dead to mass grave or left to rot.

- 224 -
And then the Oxyviva machine is found missing,
It was left at the old CCP before retreating,
Where they are now is better than before,
But the machine must be had all the more.

- 225 -
Sergeant of medics must attend with two infantry is tow,
To return the machine and give life to the low,
But RPA soldiers do block his way,
And appears to not want the Aussie to stray.

- 226 -
"We need to get inside and retrieve our apparatus,"
"No you cannot, so go away and do not berate us",
"I can see it just there and we need it, please,"
"You cannot have entry with such great ease."

- 227 -
"Shall I get help,
Or give a big yelp?"
"You cannot come in,"
And he gave a big grin.

- 228 -
"Let me in now, damn you!
We are dire and you clearly have no clue,
We need the machine now, it is important to us,
We save your people, should not it be discuss?"

- 229 -
Thirty more RPA then come out to play,
Revealed from view where they lay,
They stepped forward in display,
They are out to create dismay.

- 230 -
The sergeant sees no way out,
The RPA care not about,
The people and the UN, they are the same to them,
Just an obstacle in the way of their gem.

- 231 -
Wealth is to be had from wielding sword and shield,
They get this from conquering land and field,
All they have to do is kill the people,
Regardless of religion, or Kibeho and its temple.

- 232 -
Further afield a shot rings out,
From near hospital compound as though a great shout,
A sniper in building not far away,
Firing shots at Aussie as he may.

- 233 -
Take cover and search for the sniper,
Possibly gendarme not caring and striking like viper,
But the search reveals nought,
He is nowhere around and no longer sought.

- 234 -
The devil is fighting the Aussie from both sides,
He cannot win against these tides,
No one wants the UN here,
Not since they first appear.

- 235 -
It is an uphill battle to convince them other,
That they mean well and here to help smother,
The RPA as they commit genocide,
But in the end the people must decide.

- 236 -
Propaganda is in full swing,
It is as though the people have suffered a sting,
RPA spread false news throughout the land,
That the UN should not be allowed to demand.

KIBEHO

- 237 -
And so atrocity continues,
Creating many issues,
UN manpower is strained,
Nothing in reserve remained.

- 238 -
Not long after the sound of weapons cocking,
In some weapons the parts to rear locking,
This means bullets are ready in, or for chamber,
Ready to be fired and woken from slumber.

- 239 -
And then screams of mayhem can he heard,
The sound is reverberating in head absurd,
One to remember for all time to come,
A nightly nightmare for some when they return home.

- 240 -
There is a mother rocking a dead baby in her arms grand,
An elderly man on knees praying with Bible in hand,
Another man watches as his daughter is taken on stretcher away,
To mass grave and poor memory for him to stay.

- 241 -
A soldier scans his watch for time of day,
It is just mid morning and turning grey,
The crowd appears on edge, a reasonable reaction,
For they feel the terror of RPA retribution.

- 242 -
Retribution for what, they think they know,
Probably interahamwe in the crowd below,
Then swarms of humanity come up the slopes around,
Towards the Zambian compound on higher ground.

- 243 -
A fence of military wire forms a cordon, a caution,
A fence of strength around instils resolution,
NGOs too surrender to their hospitality,
And few are left outside the fragile neutrality.

- 244 -
Thirty RPA appear to have retreated,
But firing of weapons is now greeted,
Firing continues unabated,
The RPA are so hated.

- 245 -
A medic appears freaked,
But the good news is leaked,
"Look over there, do you see,
Our Infantry are standing ground for thee."

- 246 -
A protection of wire and infantry,
Standing guard against hostility,
They are there to stay,
They will not stray.

KIBEHO

- 247 -
Zambians stand beside the Aussie,
They act as one and mighty,
But the compound is small and cannot assist,
And so civilian in large number are desist.

- 248 -
Infantry commander tries an encouraging word,
To RPA he asks a favour be heard,
"I need to know I can retrieve the wounded,"
"No," is the reply for they care not with feet planted.

- 249 -
Gunfire continues unabated,
But still this is not heavy or related,
To evil of later today much worse,
When all moral sense departs quite terse.

- 250 -
"We need to help these people, I must insist,"
Says again the Infantry commander through mist,
The mist of brainless RPA to his front,
With not ample feeling for even a grunt.

- 251 -
But then the mist clears slightly,
RPA gives encouraging words most lightly,
"Okay, you can go if you wish,
To die out there amongst the fish."

- 252 -
Yes, they are fish in a barrel,
But the barrel is ample,
A lot of fish in a small place,
And so to help others the Infantry do race.

- 253 -
Shots ring out here and there,
A ping and a pong but soldiers do not stare,
They concentrate on the task at hand,
And act the act looked upon as grand.

- 254 -
Then out of the crowd a group of twenty or more,
Little children that anyone would adore,
They come to the compound gate as a group,
Hoping for safety to be recoup.

- 255 -
Zambian to Aussie he does translate,
"The mothers tell them to come to gate,"
"But the mothers should care for them,
We do not have room here for this handful of gem."

- 256 -
"You do not understand," says the Zambian,
"The mothers are all dead and we are now their custodian,"
And weapons continue unabated,
More children come deflated.

KIBEHO

- 257 -
An SAS man sees something out of the way,
A six year old boy to danger zone has stray,
The boy is frozen scared in danger zone ahead,
But ignore it not, for soldier does attend instead.

- 258 -
Bullets hit around him as he runs along,
A RPA man firing intently and that is wrong,
But SAS still runs to protect the child boy,
And does return with this living flesh not toy.

- 259 -
And child does not appear sad nor happy,
And he is given a seat on a truck most snappy,
The SAS waves goodbye and walks from test,
The child then falls dead with shrapnel in chest.

- 260 -
Vehicles continue to be loaded most proper,
With wounded for evac via truck or chopper,
Priority one, two or three,
Let us hope they can now live free.

- 261 -
It is just on noon when the skies embark,
A storm of the tropics does commence to turn dark,
And a chopper too from horizon does appear,
Lands on the ground and asks for medical ear.

- 262 -
A medic is there and asks what's wrong,
The pilot then gives a smirk quite strong,
"A new oxyviva machine for you if you please,
With a message of 'do not lose this one'," he does now tease.

- 263 -
And the chopper is loaded with wounded,
And a few kids once stranded,
The pilots are a courageous lot,
They do their job and never lose the plot.

- 264 -
A medic must also attend the wounded in flight,
But before they leave he is given slight fright,
He is handed many rolls of film of disgrace,
Of RPA atrocities and the filth of this place.

- 265 -
"If I get caught with this I die,"
"Then don't get caught, you must try,
For it must be delivered to appropriate hand,
For peace to one day enrich this land."

- 266 -
It is now that the chopper lifts off on its route,
And the real horror of Kibeho plays out,
What happens now is worse than ever before,
Not a single person can fathom what is in store.

KIBEHO

- 267 -
The skies above open up like removing a glove,
It is a word of disappointment from God high above,
And RPA unleash all hell,
Every kind of military shell.

- 268 -
It is now the UN and NGO act fast,
Come flooding to compound to the last,
Maybe a few are lost outside,
To help rescue them later infantry do ride.

- 269 -
Tutsi soldiers sweep the lower ground,
Killing all of those around,
One twenty thousand try to storm the compound,
UN hoping the wire holds, with infantry standing their ground.

- 270 -
Interahamwe within the crowd,
Also do horror from beneath their shroud,
They use machete and knife against IDP,
And RPA continue as though angry.

- 271 -
But the eyes of RPA reveal a truth,
It is not anger but something aloof,
They have gone insane for sure,
It is as though evil mind is allure.

- 272 -
They like their religion and bible here,
Another man is seen holding it dear,
A Tutsi soldier walks up to him now,
And gives not a furrow of the brow.

- 273 -
He looks to the Aussie guarding the compound,
And then to the old man kneeling on the ground,
The RPA smiles and points his gun,
And shoots the man dead as though a great pun.

- 274 -
But be it pun,
Or for fun,
The RPA kill,
For the thrill.

- 275 -
They invoke the Aussie to react as the old man fell,
In the hope of firing on the UN as well,
They wish to kill anyone who gets in their way,
Their very insanity has obviously gone stray.

- 276 -
Another IDP pretends to be dead,
Drags a corps upon his head,
He hides from the RPA killing machine,
They are to the core very, very mean.

KIBEHO

- 277 -
A woman is screaming in labour,
The RPA react like thunder,
A bayonet is used against the child as born,
And from the umbilical it is torn.

- 278 -
Are you sickened yet by what you read,
It is all the truth and with you I plead,
But you do not believe it, I hear you say,
To hell with you, the reader this day.

- 279 -
These things happened at Kibeho found,
More still to come quite profound,
If you do not believe... well hand back this book,
Give the words back to those forever on tenterhook.

- 280 -
The interahamwe have another name,
Like hardliner which basically means the same,
But who cares for they use children as shields,
Right there in front and upon the fields.

- 281 -
Fields of slaughter like never seen,
This ground around can now never be clean,
It has been dirtied like never before,
Surely nothing worse can be in store.

- 282 -
Bullets strike ground near the UN post,
They all go unscathed, unlike the most,
More than ten thousand people will be killed this day,
But history will deny this and agree with count in May.

- 283 -
History will scorch the truth,
Like hiding pain from sore tooth,
You can hide it but it is there,
The truth can be seen by careful and studying glare.

- 284 -
Some Aussies cock their weapons too,
What else should they do,
They fix bayonets as well,
To try and hold back the swell.

- 285 -
RPA are firing and you should protect from that,
The hardliners are vicious but hard to see without hat,
Masqueraded well, all those who have been bested,
But who is evil and who can be trusted.

- 286 -
The RPA are a threat,
And hardliners too carry their net,
IDP are harmless but dangerous,
All manner of evil out to do grievous.

KIBEHO

- 287 -
Another woman is walking along,
Dead baby in arms signing silent song,
RPA points weapon and shoots her dead,
Smile on face, his mind is easily read.

- 288 -
Aussie and Zambian have orders to adhere,
They cannot prevent this and neither their peer,
They have no power at all to act,
It is the Rules of Engagement upon them stack.

- 289 -
They are restricted to aid,
These people unpaid,
Whilst Aussie gets his wages,
For watching them he rages.

- 290 -
Minds are in turmoil,
For death is everywhere upon this bloody soil,
Paid to sit and stand tall,
They appear to do nothing at all.

- 291 -
UN soldiers start to feel dread,
"It won't be long and we'll all be dead,"
"And for doing nothing we'll all go to hell,"
"And our Kigali guys will get the same as well."

- 292 -
"Go to hell I don't care,
But to live with this guilt is unfair,
Why does the UN have these stinking rules,
Why are we all treated like fools."

- 293 -
"We are soldiers and do as we're told,
So to your actions you should not be scold,
It is not your fault what has happened,
I know your feelings have been dampened."

- 294 -
And so they do as best they can,
Working as hard as any man,
But women are no different, you hear!
Their courage should be remembered each year.

- 295 -
It is afternoon now,
And to medics all infantry bow,
The nurses and doctors work miracles,
Especially when considering their shackles.

- 296 -
Work and work all day,
No time for play,
Working fingers to the bone,
They are individuals but never alone.

KIBEHO

- 297 -
And then the medic whom was previously tasked,
Brings back the rolls of film not asked,
He couldn't offload them when landed,
And so now back they get handed.

- 298 -
Without further ado,
As though by staple or glue,
The rolls of film are taken back,
And in a pouch once more stack.

- 299 -
Do we know where those films are today,
I do not know and have to say nay,
It would be nice to see them,
Give proof as to the mayhem.

- 300 -
Treating the children appears to be worse,
Why should they have to suffer this curse,
Why should a child have to suffer RPA ill wish,
Because they are like others in barrel of fish.

- 301 -
Mid afternoon and the firing does continue,
It's as though the RPA have no clue,
How can they not see or understand,
What they do is but like… contraband.

- 302 -
And very young children carry guns too,
They also commit atrocities and add to the stew,
They are bullied into doing some killing,
Regardless of whether or not they are willing.

- 303 -
Children soldiers appear the worse,
What would mothers say if not provide curse,
How can a dear child sin this way,
How can they kill and then stay.

- 304 -
Stay to do more of the same,
Kill for the thrill of the game,
Because they are brainwashed for sure,
The RPA have them in their lure.

- 305 -
The SAS WO has again arrived in chopper,
Landed to take more back as is proper,
"Looks like you guys need me here,
I have to stay," and so unloaded his gear.

- 306 -
The chopper pilot hears a nearby ping,
Possibly RPA shooting at chopper a sin,
Maybe ricochet, but he puts it from mind,
And continues amidst prayer with the grind.

KIBEHO

- 307 -
Another mass breakout is under way,
Thousands of innocent again go stray,
For chanting is going on in the church,
The RPA in great number ready to lurch.

- 308 -
Dozens of RPA burst from the building,
This is the height of the great massacring,
Thousands are killed like a hammer,
RPA pounding away without stammer.

- 309 -
No pause in the slaughter,
But from some RPA a little laughter,
Everything you read before,
Is now repeated all the more.

- 310 -
What you have read before is repeated now,
Slaughtering people as though a cow,
Lambs to the slaughter again, and now thrice,
Nothing but meat to be sliced and diced.

- 311 -
The chopper pilot to soldier does say,
As they begin to be underway,
"If you hear a ping you must let me know,
The chopper may be hit but accustomed to sound I grow."

- 312 -
"I thought that was only in the picture show,"
Replies the soldiers now in the know,
"The RPA shoot anywhere for they do not care,
I am surprised they haven't tried a flare."

- 313 -
With 22 wounded awaiting on truck,
Ready for another evac with good luck,
The choppers are coming much more often,
It is a never ending cycle that does not soften.

- 314 -
It is mid afternoon and a report rather gripping,
It appears an MSF doctor or nurse is missing,
It comes to ear that she hid in a cupboard,
Not far from Zambian compound and out to starboard.

- 315 -
MSF is Doctors Without Borders,
Whom attend the needy without military orders,
But when times run foul you hear admittance,
And to grant them safety they require assistance.

- 316 -
So military personal are needed,
To orders they are heeded,
It is not a Nazi Party daughter,
But even they would receive aid from slaughter.

- 317 -
You can not find racial hatred amongst the UN here,
Aussie soldiers for most do steer,
Away from tormenting foreigners as though task,
With job to do they freely give regardless of mask.

- 318 -
Aussie commander will not leave in lurch,
"You two follow me and help with the search,
We must go and find this woman so woven,
The one of good character, which she has proven."

- 319 -
Bullets strike the ground as they move,
Great power of courage they do prove,
But find her they do in hiding,
Crying but safe with future abiding.

- 320 -
Another turn for the worse does now appear,
RPA on two spurs with crossfire adhere,
2,000 IDP go astray,
Trying to run and to get away.

- 321 -
Rocket propelled grenade,
50 calibre machine gun made,
Hand held weapons galore,
Pick off victims as thou seashells from shore.

- 322 -
Hundreds fall to their death fast,
Continuing to try for safety at last,
Which they see as the Zambian compound,
Which is small and has little ground.

- 323 -
One IDP is on the wire,
Pleads for life he does desire,
He offers soldiers a great wad of money,
But today no bee would be enticed by honey.

- 324 -
"Your money is no good,
And I am not in the mood,
Put it quickly away,
That is all I can say."

- 325 -
Then he thrusts forward a young girl,
Another of long hair and slight curl,
In broken English he does explain,
"Take her and entry here I gain."

- 326 -
He wants to exchange the child,
"She good for you and mild,
She will please you and more,
Do all of your chore."

KIBEHO

- 327 -
No more can the soldier take,
And removes the IDP first rate,
Takes him to the rear near fence,
And from there does dispense.

- 328 -
The man understands clearly and sure,
He cannot make a bargain, not lure,
And he runs down the road away from the scene,
And then you can hear him obscene.

- 329 -
A scream comes to his lips most grisly,
As RPA swarm upon him most quickly,
They drag him from view and away,
Rifle shot and machete then finish off their prey.

- 330 -
The Aussie soldier goes back to his chore,
Unsure what that entails anymore,
There is simply too many to save, it is a disgrace,
Too much suffering in this one single place.

- 331 -
Aussie soldier comes across ill fate,
But he at least is not too late,
A young child with half her face torn away,
Scared to move she intends to stay.

- 332 -
The Aussie soldier will give her aid,
With great ambition they are made,
They move her away with great care,
Taking her away whilst under RPA glare.

- 333 -
The RPA are the Devil,
And they are most evil,
But Christian crucifix some do display,
How can they possibly live this way.

- 334 -
And pilot from chopper takes to the air,
The last this day he has done his fair share,
He looks down below and sees one hundred more,
Being shot dead as they try to escape what's in store.

- 335 -
And as the dark of night does arrive,
The UN gives orders to get in trucks and drive,
Aussie soldier cannot stay here this night,
It would be to the RPA delight.

- 336 -
Aussie is here to provide security to medic,
And that is the only task quite tragic,
So much more they could be doing right now,
But restraint is all that meets their furrowed brow.

KIBEHO

- 337 -
And then one last task is met with fast,
NGO and UNAMIR to the last,
Gather as many babies as they can,
So they can depart with them in van.

- 338 -
And as they move fast away, they come under glare,
The screams of the dying and suffering fills the air,
It is a disgrace that they should be left like this,
This is the UN which none will ever miss.

Kibeho Camp is a scene of utter devastation. Bodies lying everywhere, all manner of injuries evident. Wailing and moaning fills the air. There are several trucks in the background being driven away, RPA trucks filled to the brim with corpses, removed in order to deny, or lighten, any accusation of genocide and massacre.

Sunday 23rd April, 0630hrs.

KIBEHO

- 339 -
The killing appears to have finished,
Met its end after being well dished,
It is now time to clean up the mess,
A task met by those I'm sure you can guess.

- 340 -
The CCP is set up superbly but once again,
The aftermath of violence an unnecessary stain,
Most of those present feel ashamed for leaving,
And now they see before them thousands of grieving.

- 341 -
A body count is needed for history to ridicule,
And so men in teams commence with the schedule,
One counter for the dead,
The other for those requiring bed.

- 342 -
Teams of stretchers will do the rest,
Gathering the wounded and do their best,
Medics will work as hard to day,
As they did before during these final days before May.

- 343 -
And even as they do their count,
Can be seen many bodies commencing to mount,
Onto trucks preparing to take dead away,
As RPA finalise the obscurity of their stay.

- 344 -
The RPA will take them from view,
Somewhere far where mass graves grew,
Only educated guess will provide the real number,
As to true numbers of massacred now forever in slumber.

- 345 -
Two teams under the SAS do their duty,
Crossing the ground around so dirty,
Literally dozens upon dozens of living babies,
Still strapped to their mother's backs once ladies.

- 346 -
But corpses they are now, though with babies alive,
Take them to an orphanage in order to thrive,
The RPA were always keen to kill babies before,
But these dozens escaped the mass body store.

- 347 -
Even said surely, another grave is dug,
The dead deposited, no ceremonious hug,
Just picked up and dropped as though carcass of meat,
For Mr. Death is waiting with grin to greet.

- 348 -
Dozens of babies also sit alone,
Too small a weapon target even to be shot at whilst prone,
All picked up and carried away,
A minor victory during these days of darkest grey.

KIBEHO

- 349 -
An Aussie grunt comes across mountains of trash,
Blue sheets once tents from NGO stash,
It appears to be moving from underneath,
And so he looks under and immediately feels a little relief.

- 350 -
Two babies laying next to mother,
Both mothers dead and so clearly not brother,
But they are like twins these two he sees,
For they share everything alike on this ground without trees.

- 351 -
Another soldiers sees a young child,
Sitting alone in mud and appearing rather mild,
Just looking around with nothing to say,
Even one so young is suffering in dismay.

- 352 -
He carries child along towards CCP,
Past mass grave in which he can see,
Masses of dead very cold and all sightless,
Limbs interlocked with flies harvesting lifeless.

- 353 -
The word is passed around and hence beneath rubbish all search,
And to the glory of God many children favoured by church,
Picked from the ground, happy to take child into grasp,
To the waiting hand of medics whom all give a gasp.

- 354 -
The dead are easy to attend,
A short trip to grave will mend,
But so many will take forever to move,
And so the infantry must push and get into a grove.

- 355 -
Stretchers working hour after hour,
Bodies to mass grave before they go sour,
Pile them up high so you do not have to suffer,
By filling that grave and then digging another.

- 356 -
The children are managed well,
Even though a tide which seems to swell,
Now looking beneath plastic sheeting too,
The soldiers here find plenty to do.

- 357 -
The living are hardest to deal with here,
Most are wounded severely from tow to ear,
But where can they be found do I hear,
Well quite frankly they are very near.

- 358 -
Almost two thousand have congregate at the MSF compound,
Now a safe haven from which RPA are expelled from ground,
This is near Zambian muster of which we spoke,
And all soldiers here are UN, and if not medic, then good bloke.

KIBEHO

- 359 -
Alas the wounded whom cannot move, since yesterday's rain,
Suffer out in the grounds around in great pain,
Aussies and Zambian will get to them sooner or later,
And this is the most important and of all tasks the greater.

- 360 -
And word soon arrives that RPA are not happy,
They insist under force that the body count stops snappy,
No longer are they permitted to count the number of dead,
Forced to put away their pace counters in pocket instead.

- 361 -
And even after such a short time,
Over 4,000 dead are counted amongst grime,
650 are wounded and will be got to safety later,
If RPA do not manage to mince them with machete like grater.

- 362 -
Two young children are taken to surgeon table,
One has severe bleeding to neck and the other is stable,
"Put that one inside and we will tend to it soon,
Put the other outside to its ultimate doom."

- 363 -
"But it's a child and needs to be attended,
We can not leave it as though stranded",
The WO SAS stands his ground well,
"Do as you are told, good man, and then take a spell."

- 364 -
"We can only save those whom can be saved,
Others must be allowed to meet the grave,
I don't like to pick and choose,
But we too are here as though with neck in noose."

- 365 -
"It is filthy work and a great mess,
But decisions must be made no less,
If you have oxygen for one and the other must die,
Then an educated decision I make with no lie."

- 366 -
"I shall live with my decisions knowing I did best,
For that one there will not pass the test,
But this child may grow to be important one day,
I must tell myself its future is not grey."

- 367 -
And so this is how they must look at it when they nurture,
As though the decisions made are for bold future,
Those suffering here amongst this filth and decay,
Will recall its horror and make Rwanda a better place to stay.

- 368 -
And now they start referring to all patients less formal,
Taking away all feeling of being remorseful,
The patient is no longer referred to as human, but instead,
"That leg," "That arm," "That gash wound to head."

- 369 -
By midday all appears to be working reasonably well,
The wounded being sorted despite mass a great swell,
Choppers are landing and taking away,
All those able to be mended with hospital stay.

- 370 -
Those that are capable,
And appear more stable,
Are put onto truck,
And with them good luck.

- 371 -
One chopper lands and a patient near loaded,
When RPA commander comes running astounded,
"That person cannot go" says he,
"Why not?" asks the SAS next to patient on knee.

- 372 -
"She is Hutu and must stay here,"
SAS now stands and does so peer,
Into the eye of RPA commander,
Gives his opinion without slander.

- 373 -
"She doesn't look Hutu to me,"
"She is, for I can see,"
And now he tries his horrendous best,
For RPA replies with most moral test.

- 374 -
The RPA thrusts forward a young child,
"You can take for the old women this young boy so mild,"
It is a trade pure and simple in which to agree,
"Give him the woman and get the child quickly."

- 375 -
And another surprise RPA does tell,
"You will take this man here as well,"
Says SAS: "He doesn't look wounded to me,"
"Take him not and no one will, you'll see."

- 376 -
And so exchange is made,
Probably a better trade,
For the old woman was dying,
And the young child no need relying.

- 377 -
The chopper takes off and then another is seen,
Coming in slow and then to starboard does lean,
The Minister for Justice and Interior whom no one applaud,
And the Head of Human Rights Mission whom here is stored.

- 378 -
Mr. Khan is there also,
And all appear to be aglow,
For after they land they all shake the hand,
With the most evil RPA so grand.

KIBEHO

- 379 -
They now move away from Landing Zone,
And towards the killing fields of which RPA do not atone,
They await another man who will soon appear,
Rwandan President Pasteur Bizimunga to whom Aussies sneer.

- 380 -
They move as a group before the French they grill,
Where little church sits upon hill,
Mr. Khan sees clearly of the ground and the gore,
The Frenchman: "Our reports show 2,000 dead and more."

- 381 -
Captain Roberts also has his say,
Bizimunga replies: "This number is grey,
It is far too many for what really does appear,
The true figure is only 330 deaths here."

- 382 -
Khan says: "No sir, I cannot agree, for that is slander",
Bizimunga then speaks to RPA commander,
"Is it true IDP fired upon your men without end,"
"Yes it is true and we have right to defend."

- 383 -
And UN member, Captain Francis, is forced to defend,
To uphold all against this negative trend,
"The slaughter here has been extremely exhausting,
The figures I have shown you are what I am reporting."

- 384 -
Bizimunga listens to argument,
And decision put into cement,
"So Captain Francis, it was you and your men,
And all of the UN whom have sown untruth then."

- 385 -
"You have my reports," says Francis in defence,
"I have disclosed and provided all good sense,
You see the mass graves all around,
I have personally counted 1,500 on this ground."

- 386 -
Bizimunga looks at Francis with great intent,
He says quite clearly: "You are impotent,"
And so the truth is covered and nipped in the bud,
Accusations of genocide sinking as though in mud.

- 387 -
One more chopper comes into view,
Carrying Aussie CO and RSM into the stew,
CNN and BBC reporters in the mix,
All come to get their daily fix.

- 388 -
Bizimunga is close by Aussie commander,
Who hears their great slander,
Bizimunga says to Minister: "I know how,
There is a way to stop the media now."

KIBEHO

- 389 -
"We must stand by our estimate in number,
Never give an inch or talk of this in slumber,"
"I agree fully," replies the Minister for Justice,
"And for your service you will no longer be novice."

- 390 -
All from the chopper now attend the CCP,
And they do so with rapidly, dissipating glee,
One reporter says: "Looks like you guys are busy,"
But that sounds rather pathetic and greasy.

- 391 -
If you have nothing important to say,
Then out of their hair you must stay,
Medics are as busy as nest-building larks,
No time for silly quotation remarks.

- 392 -
No need to say, 'nice weather today',
As though nothing out of ordinary lay,
But from another a more reliant question does appear,
"How have you guys been busy whilst you have been here?"

- 393 -
"The days did seem to get worse,
And with them we grew terse,
Only now is it getting quiet,
Outside is no longer a riot."

- 394 -
Five more patients appear at the door,
"My God!" says one of them as he sees the gore,
But he has seen nothing at all to be aghast,
The truth of the horror has already passed.

- 395 -
Some of those whom do the least dirty work,
Try to claw their persona from the murk,
They do not like to be left behind,
For the sake of feeling, for the sake of mind.

- 396 -
The RSM gets his video camera out of pouch,
"I'll give you $300 a foot," says one, out of touch,
The reporter seems more interest in funding college for daughter,
Not in the sheer horror and the abysmal slaughter.

- 397 -
And then a Captain with pips on shoulder,
New Task Commander to the scene, appears to be bolder,
Gives order for medic to find more casualties,
Looking most important amidst the formalities.

- 398 -
"Yes sir," says Sergeant medic at once so not to deny,
"Come and I'll show you more," says Captain not shy,
"We have 2,000 IDPs that won't be reared,
We have tried all we can but they are scared."

- 399 -
One reporter requests they take a look,
And for this great advantage the captain took,
"Come with me and I'll show more,
I'll try and be informative, that is for sure."

- 400 -
And RSM sees soldiers work with great respect,
Responsibility for which they do not neglect,
"Do the men get much of a break,"
"About two minutes every hour they take."

- 401 -
They do not like to stop working,
For they feel the people need rejoicing,
They try to do justice to humanity,
Especially amongst all this insanity.

- 402 -
At the water point all go to work,
Gathering wounded from the murk,
Medic sees a newborn baby there bound,
Its stomach appearing swollen and round.

- 403 -
He picks up the young one and turns,
Return to post, for post he now yearns,
A Rwandan jumps out in front of him,
Head wound severe but okay at the limb.

- 404 -
He staggers a little here,
And the shock in his eyes is clear,
His brains are exposed,
Blood covering his face and nose.

- 405 -
But he appears to be walking alright,
But then staggers a little to right,
He appears sick in the eye,
He is priority one, don't deny.

- 406 -
Medic looks at him hard,
"He's priority one to inch and yard,
We can only save those whom we can save,
But this poor fellow has already entered the grave."

- 407 -
The man goes down on his knees,
Hands together in prayer he pleas,
The Aussie shakes his mind from obscurity,
Another victim then approaches medic and security.

- 408)
She is hobbling along,
But appears strong,
A gun wound to the leg,
She has no cause to beg.

KIBEHO

- 409 -
Medic orders infantry to assist,
And then from a decision does desist,
"If the man with head wound can walk,
Then to aid him we all can talk."

- 410 -
The soldiers convince the man to walk,
"This way, this way, do not stand there like stork,"
And slowly he moves but he does the job,
And walks to aid not much farther than stones lob.

- 411 -
Back at the evacuation post,
Security do loading the most,
Mostly by truck without delay,
People are loaded to sit and to lay.

- 412 -
A woman is loaded with glee,
Shot once in each knee,
Another one sitting at her side,
Gunshot to ankle, prepares for ride.

- 413 -
Medic Sergeant reports his find,
That only a few can be found from behind,
But there should be more there still,
It appears like failure and makes one ill.

- 414 -
"Water point is clear with no one to be found,
I have searched all over the ground,"
And reality strikes hard as all know the truth,
RPA have removed the evidence to remain aloof.

- 415 -
And Zambian advises with misgiving,
That RPA bury the living,
Some find this absurd,
Others of it before have heard.

- 416 -
And Zambian points to area all know,
Where RPA mass graves grow,
It is here they bury the living,
It is here they gift misgiving.

- 417 -
So the Zambian pulls the medic aside,
"There is still time to prepare more for ride,
Several spaces now vacant for some have since died,
Search for more patients we all must stride."

- 418 -
And medic to Captain once more does attend,
Medic wishes to try and amend,
To have every inch of the truck filled,
For the RPA want everyone milled.

- 419 -
"We do not have time right now,
To the remainder of the day we must bow,"
"But all I need is a little more time,
Instead of burying dead with lime."

- 420 -
"No more Sergeant, for there is no time,
Let us finish with today's grime,
Load all you can and let's be on our way,
Being here longer will not aid our Rwandan stay."

- 421 -
"We have to attend our chores and our choices,
Instead of in our heads hearing voices,"
And voice does now enter the medic's head,
As though written on paper and easily read.

- 422 -
"Please sir, just a few minutes more,
A few children I saw just past water store,"
Captain looks at watch and appears very stern,
"Ten minutes more and you must return."

- 423 -
Meanwhile a few priority one need flight,
But RSM and CO are ready to say good night,
So IDP in need do high rank replace,
This is nothing at all, it's not a disgrace.

- 424 -
For another chopper will show its face soon,
To fill a quota and release some from gloom,
High rank have jobs of importance to attend,
Those of priority one are taken in the end.

- 425 -
It is almost dark here now,
Amongst the rolling hills all bow,
Looking towards the horizon it appears to tease,
The sun disappearing solemnly if you please.

- 426 -
So medic is on mission once more,
To save children only from the gore,
"You infantry look as hard as you can,
Leave no space on truck, and no child is ban."

- 427 -
"Look under everything you see,
Try and move heaven we must agree,
Do all we can to save the younger generation,
I heard one earlier, no illusion."

- 428 -
And rubbish is thrown aside without rest,
Blue sheeting lifted to hopefully reveal a nest,
"STOP and listen quietly you must,
I hear something and in that I trust."

- 429 -
And after a very short search,
A child is finally taken with a lurch,
"Let's get back as quick as we can,
No time to waste we must stick to the plan."

- 430 -
The last of the patients is secured on truck,
Hope isn't assured but with them good luck,
Give them good chance and avoid all strife,
Hope they live long and prosper in life.

During the events at Kibeho, between the 18th and the 23rd of April, 1995, more than 10,000 IDPs lost their lives.

The MSF compound contains 1,500+ IDPs crammed in vile circumstances; they stubbornly refused to leave for fear of their lives.

On Thursday 27th April, Rwanda's President, His Excellency Pasteur Bizimunga, accuses the international community of giving false numbers on the deaths at Kibeho. The official figure accepted by the Rwandan government is estimated at 338 deaths.

> Tuesday, 9th May 1340hrs.

At precisely 1:40pm, on Tuesday, 9th May, 1995; the last 546 IDPs depart the compound. The camp is cleared and the Australian Contingent concludes its operation at Kibeho.

KIBEHO

Carol Louise Vaughan-Evans
Royal Australian Army Medical Corps
Medal for Gallantry

Lieutenant Thomas Steven Tilbrook
Royal Australian Infantry Corps
Medal for Gallantry

Warrant Officer Class Two Roderick Malcolm Scott
Special Air Service Regiment
Medal for Gallantry

Lance Corporal Andrew Colin Miller
Royal Australian Infantry Corps
Medal for Gallantry

LEST WE FORGET

My personal description of some individuals is derived from experience and may not have been experienced by others. Opinions are also derived from recorded events as seen through the eyes of others. I have also done what I believe is my best in writing this poem, though I have limited experience with poetry and limited schooling.

All written here is true but I have heard of people laughing at it in disbelief, as with the paramedic from Australia who accused some infantry soldiers of rorting the system and claiming to have PTSD when in fact they don't, as through his eyes we all should have been trained to a degree that we could have stomach what occurred during those weeks of mayhem, for he clearly believes that he has seen as much as a paramedic on the streets of the suburbs. His accusations have hurt many people. Quite a few personnel have committed suicide over the years due to their involvement with the incidents at Kibeho.

Everyone is born differently and have varied limits and abilities. Someone with an IQ of 140 should not necessarily be classed as being a good achiever and a person in possession of 90 a poor good-for-nothing. We are, so I believe, all born with different traits, and if you are lucky enough to be born with an IQ of 140, should you necessarily see that as a free ticket to brag about it? A Politician, CEO, or leader in their field of expertise, is no better than an autistic child, they are simply fortunate to be born with a mind that functions well.

The breaking strain of a cord of rope is as varied as its length.

www.ingramcontent.com/pod-product-compliance
Lightning Source LLC
Chambersburg PA
CBHW020328010526
44107CB00054B/2016